HOW TO PLAY THE TROMBONE

A Step-by-Step Guide to Learning the Basics, Reading Music and Playing Songs with Audio Recordings

Text Copyright © Lightbulb Publishing

All rights reserved. No part of this guide may be reproduced in any form without permission in writing from the publisher except in the case of brief quotations embodied in critical articles or reviews.

Legal & Disclaimer

The information contained in this book and its contents is not designed to replace or take the place of any form of medical or professional advice; and is not meant to replace the need for independent medical, financial, legal or other professional advice or services, as may be required. The content and information in this book has been provided for educational and entertainment purposes only.

The content and information contained in this book has been compiled from sources deemed reliable, and it is accurate to the best of the Author's knowledge, information, and belief. However, the Author cannot guarantee its accuracy and validity and cannot be held liable for any errors and/or omissions. Further, changes are periodically made to this book as and when needed. Where appropriate and/or necessary, you must consult a professional (including but not limited to your doctor, attorney, financial advisor or such other professional advisor) before using any of the suggested remedies, techniques, or information in this book.

Upon using the contents and information contained in this book, you agree to hold harmless the Author from and against any damages, costs, and expenses, including any legal fees potentially resulting from the application of any of the information provided by this book. This disclaimer applies to any loss, damages or injury caused by the use and application, whether directly or indirectly, of any advice or information presented, whether for breach of contract, tort, negligence, personal injury, criminal intent, or under any other cause of action.

You agree to accept all risks of using the information presented in this book.

You agree that by continuing to read this book, where appropriate and/or necessary, you shall consult a professional (including but not limited to your doctor, attorney, or financial advisor or such other advisor as needed) before using any of the suggested remedies, techniques, or information in this book.

Table of Contents

PART ONE

Chapter 1: Introduction 1

    Welcome! 1

    How to Use This Book 3

Chapter 2: Instrument Basics 5

    Types of Trombones 5

    Anatomy & Assembly 8

Chapter 3: Preparing to Play 13

    Stance and grip 13

    Air, air, air 14

    Embouchure and Mouthpiece Placement 14

    The slide positions 17

    Understanding the Staff 19

PART TWO

Chapter 4: First notes 21

    The note F, E♭, D, C & B♭ 21

    First Song 27

    The note G 27

    Twinkle Twinkle Little Star 28

The note A & B♭ 29

Another Piece 31

B♭ scale 32

Chapter 5: Next Steps and Beyond 33

Low A and Middle C..33

Fearless High Notes 36

Middle D and Beyond, Low G and F 36

Tempo 39

Chapter 6: More to play 41

Glissing and Lip Slurs 41

Saints...43

Chapter 7: More Theory and the Musical Alphabet 45

Slide Position Chart...45

Sharps and Flats 46

Tips for Reading Notes 46

Using the F-trigger 47

Visualizing Rhythm 47

More Musical Markings 48

PART THREE

Chapter 8: General Info 51

Troubleshooting 51

Purchasing a Trombone 52

General Care & Deep Cleaning...54

Mutes..55

Breathing Exercises 60

Chapter 9: Send Off 61

Artists to Discover 61

Learning Music by Ear..62

Conclusion... **63**

Throughout this book there are musical examples and audio recordings to follow along with on your journey to learn how to play the Trombone.

Whenever you see the following outline:

> **Listening Example #1: Note F**

Please follow along with the recordings at the Sound Cloud link below or search on Sound Cloud for "How to Play the Trombone".

https://soundcloud.com/jason_randall/sets/how-to-play-the-trombone

Part One

Chapter 1

Introduction

Welcome!

So you have decided that you want to learn the trombone! Versatile across many genres, the trombone is suitable for musicians of all ages and experiences.

Perhaps you are testing the waters to see if the trombone is right for you. Maybe you are a returning trombonist, or you already play an instrument and looking to learn another. You may be an accomplished music teacher seeking broader knowledge across the many musical instruments. Or, you are ready and eager to start learning your first instrument! Whatever experience level you are at, this book will show you what you need to know to build a solid foundation and begin your musical journey.

Evolving from the early conical trumpets, the trombone has roots stretching back to the 15th century. The early form of the instrument used to be referred to as the *sackbut*, and the trombone is one of the oldest instruments that has remained essentially unchanged over time. Fun fact: the French word for paperclip is "Trombone"! It comes from the likeness of the twisted shape of the paperclip to that of the trombone 📎

Because the trombone creates sound using the player's breath, it is considered a wind instrument, more specifically, a member of the "brass" instrument family. Aside from often being made of brass, the distinguishing feature of brass instruments is that the sound is created by a "buzz" of the player's lip. This is achieved by the cup-like mouthpiece that allows control of the lips' vibrations as the player blows into the instrument. Other popular brass instruments include the trumpet, french horn, and tuba. The trombone is somewhat unique to those instruments however—while most wind instruments use buttons and keys to sound the different notes, the trombone uses a mechanism unlike any other, the telescoping slide!

We will begin by learning the basics and becoming familiar with the instrument. Once we understand the trombone's physical features, we will blow our first notes, starting slow and progressing steadily. As we learn the instrument note by note, we will also expand our knowledge of the musical building blocks along the way, exploring each new musical element or technique with it's own unique piece. Before long, you will be playing your first song, reading and interpreting music notation! Keep in mind that the learning process can sometimes feel tedious, and that brass instruments can be particularly unforgiving at times regardless of skill level. Remember to enjoy the process of learning, and that your patience and persistence will be worth it!

Introduction

How to Use This Book

Set up partly as a play-along practice and part bite-sized music encyclopedia, this book contains all the information you need to begin learning how to play the trombone. That said, there's no better way to learn any instrument than hearing it played live in person or recorded. For this book, you can follow along with the exercises using the audio examples found here:

https://soundcloud.com/jason_randall/sets/how-to-play-the-trombone

OR

search on Sound Cloud for "How to Play the Trombone".

This author highly recommends seeking live performances in your town or city and exploring recorded music on your favorite streaming platform. Recommended listening can be found in Chapter 9. Finding your tastes and being inspired by the vast world of trombone and music is all part of the process.

Chapter 2

Instrument Basics

Types of Trombones

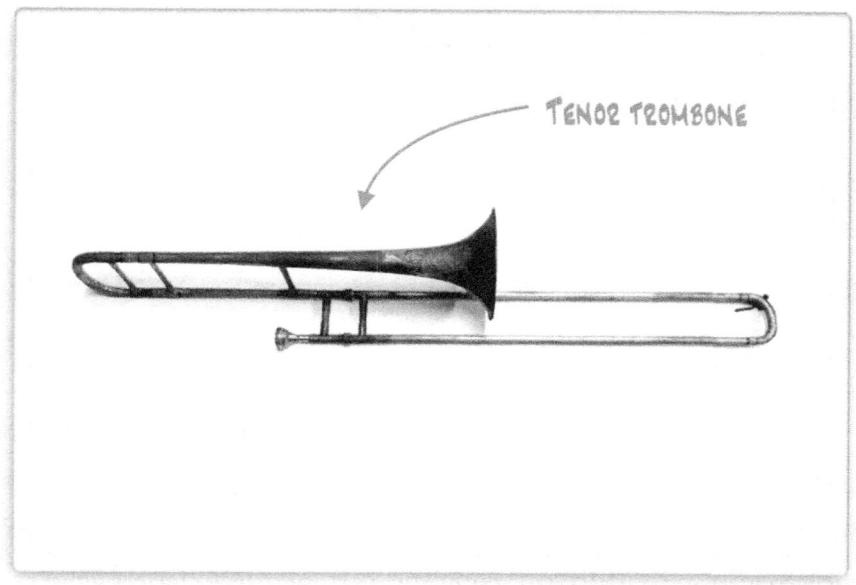

Above is a typical "tenor" trombone, great for beginners and also used by pop, rock and jazz musicians. This is the simplest type of trombone. It's essentially one long tube from end to end! Some tenor trombones have additional tubing and switches attached, like the one pictured below:

How to Play the Trombone

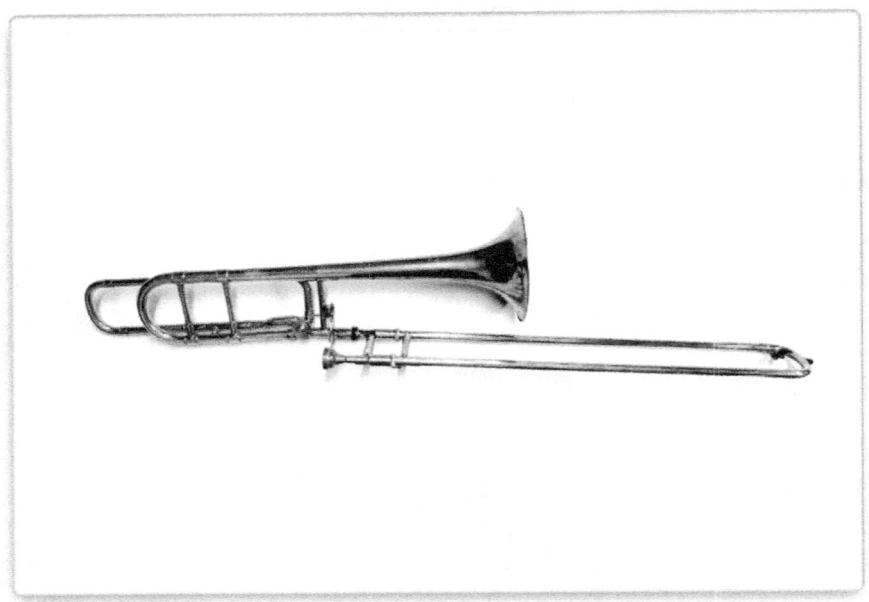

These trombones with a "trigger" look more complex but are fundamentally the same instrument. Commonly used in classical music, these tend to be slightly bigger than the standard "straight" tenor trombone. (More on using the F-trigger in Chapter 7)

The trombone below has even more tubing and size added to it and has changed character enough to be considered a different instrument: The "bass" trombone. These are specialized instruments primarily designed to play low notes, just like a tuba. They are considerably bigger, often featuring more tubing with two or more extra triggers and switches.

Instrument Basics

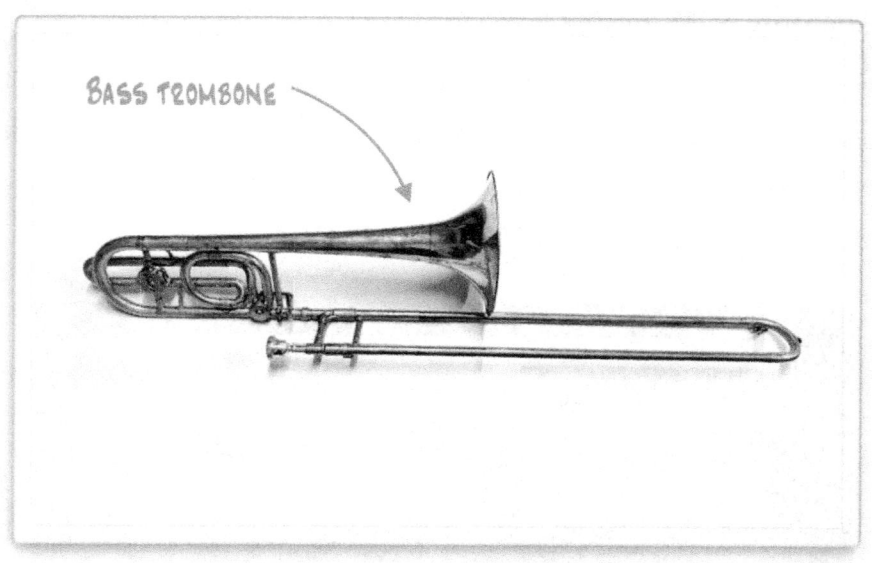

There are even more types of trombones. The alto trombone may look like an ordinary tenor but is much smaller. Even further down in size, there are soprano trombones that look like little toys, but those trombones remain rare. This author encourages you to explore the fun world of quirky-sized instruments on your own. For this book, we will focus on the tenor trombone, the most common and a great starting point for people coming to the instrument.

Getting the right trombone in good condition is important, but as long as the instrument is visibly clean, in good shape, and the slide moves freely, you're ready to play! Be sure to pick up a bottle or tube of slide oil when you get your trombone. If you would like to know more about purchasing instruments and the various makes and models, see Chapter 8.

Anatomy & Assembly

As you open the case to reveal the instrument inside, you'll notice that the trombone is broken up into three components: The bell, slide and mouthpiece. Although the trombone is a long and bulky instrument, it dismantles and is portable.

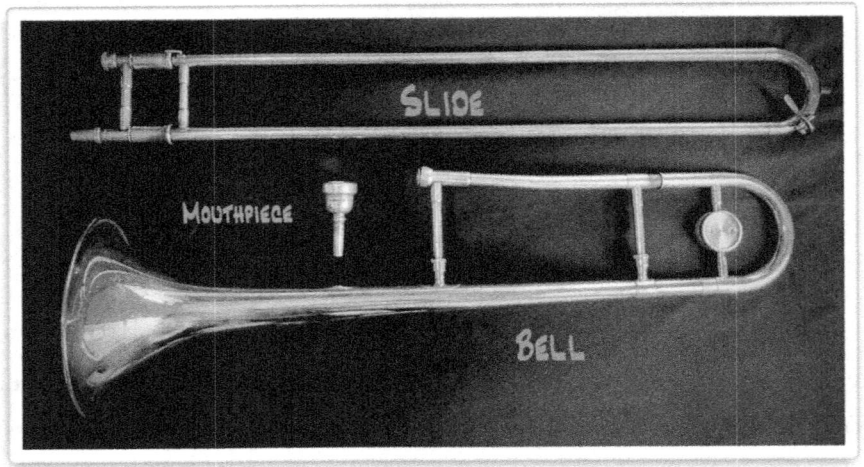

To put the instrument together:

1) Combine the slide section with the bell as shown below:

A screw nut usually joins these two components. The nut needn't be too tight, just secure enough that the bell & slide don't move under their own weight. Look down the slide from a top-down perspective and secure it at a right angle. Take note that all trombones are set up to be right-handed (Controlling the slide with the right hand), even for those who are left-handed.

Instrument Basics

2) Drop the mouthpiece in. No force is required

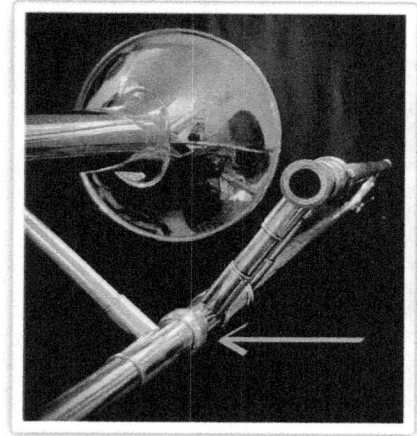
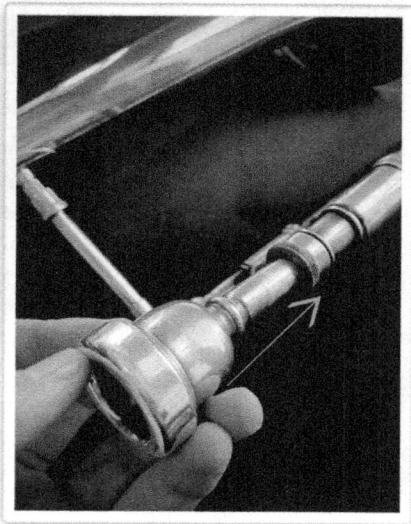

Before you play:

- Be careful with the slide; it is vulnerable to dents.

- You should apply some slide oil so that the slide can move smoothly and freely. Follow the instructions on your bottle label; the basic principle is to apply a little bit to the *inner* tube. Remember that a little oil goes a long way, and a spray of water helps too if you have a small spray bottle handy. Ideally, your slide should be slick enough to have no resistance to movement.

How to Play the Trombone

You'll notice that each component breaks down further into smaller parts. It's handy to know what some of these parts are called.

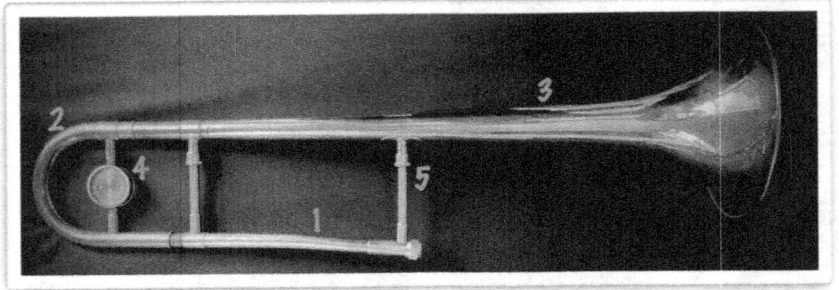

1) Goose neck
2) Tuning slide
3) Bell
4) Counter weight
5) Brace

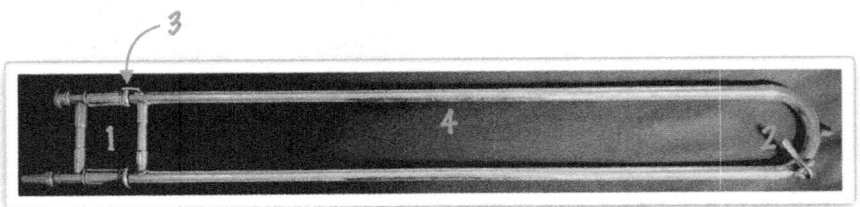

1) Slide braces
2) Water key
3) Slide lock
4) Outer slide

- Keep an eye on the tuning slide. You'll notice that just like the main slide, it telescopes, albeit with more resistance. You want this slide to be pulled out to around one inch/two-three centimeters. This sets the fine-tuning of the instrument. If the tuning slide is stiff, it can be smoothened with tuning slide grease (not to be confused with slide oil).

Instrument Basics

The water key (sometimes flagrantly referred to as the "spit valve") is there to release water inside the instrument, which is usually a build-up of the condensation from your breath. If you hear some bubbling noises as you play, that's your cue to release some of that moisture.

Chapter 3

Preparing to Play

Stance and grip

An important thing to remember is to stay physically and mentally relaxed while playing. Tension should be minimal, feeling only maybe a little sense of *compression* in your mouth as you blow.

Whether you're sitting or standing, having a relaxed and straight posture helps. As you play, the angle of the trombone should remain fairly straight, pointing out away from your body. There is some flexibility here based on personal comfort, but a general rule is that the instrument should shoot straight out of your face and body when starting.

Holding the trombone:

How to Play the Trombone

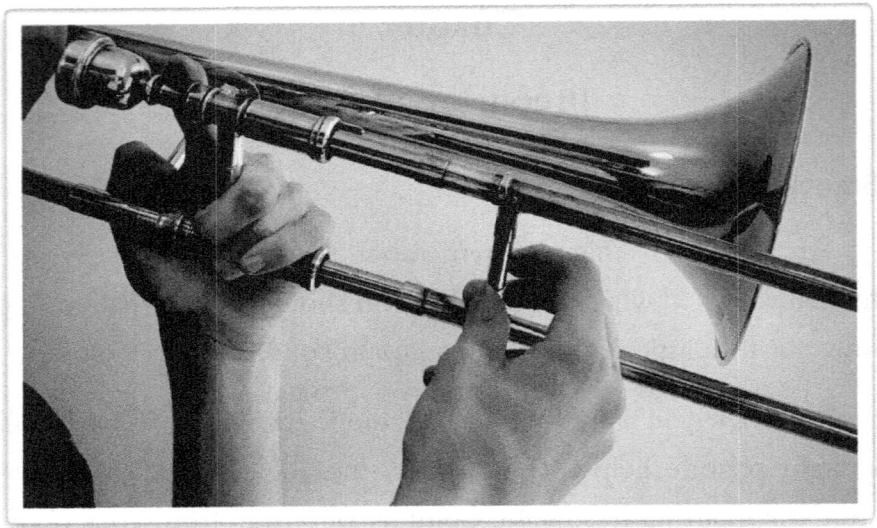

Air, air, air

Your breath is key as a trombonist.

- A big, relaxed intake of air before blowing each note is paramount. As you take a breath, mouth the the word "Whole" and fill your lungs up like a balloon

- The same idea goes for blowing the air back out: Relaxed! Imagine that you are blowing out *warm air*, smoothly and assuredly

Extra breathing exercises and tips can be found in Chapter 8.

Embouchure and Mouthpiece Placement

The shape you make with your mouth as it meets the mouthpiece is called your *embouchure* (om-ber-sure, as in "sure" enough). The sound of the trombone is the sound of your lips

Preparing to Play

vibrating, caused by the air pushing through your closed lips. Gaining good control of your lips (i.e. forming a solid embouchure) against your airflow (breath) is the aim of the game.

Here are some general tips to follow to form a good embouchure:

- To form the shape of the mouth, say "Mmmmm"

- Keep the corners of your mouth tight

- Keep your cheeks taut and refrain puffing out

- Relax your jaws and keep your teeth slightly open

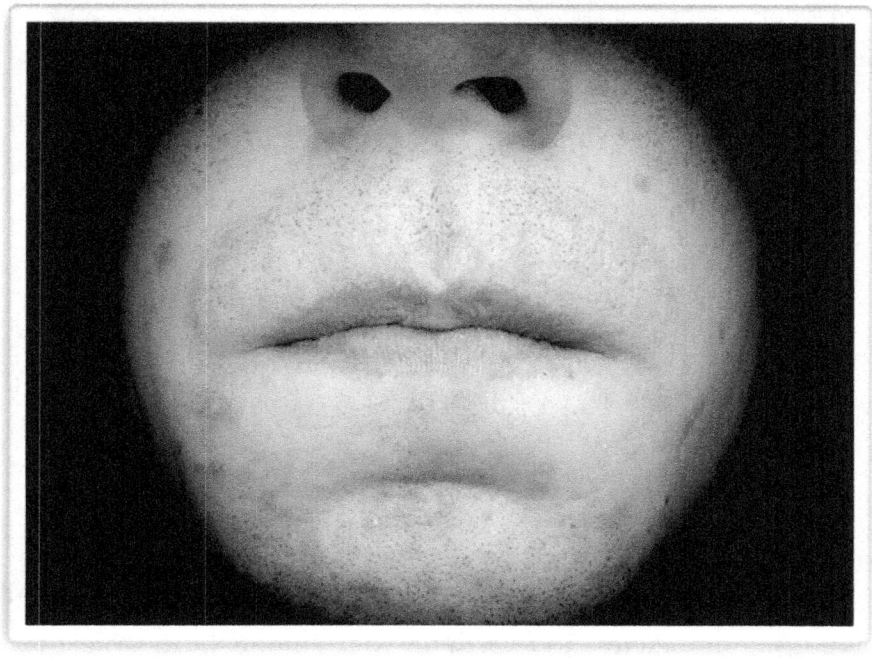

A good rule is to place the mouthpiece right in the middle, centered across your upper and lower lip. Some players prefer to place their mouthpiece covering a little more of their upper or lower lip, but this is a personal comfort choice that you will find yourself naturally gravitate toward as you play more. Keep your chin flat as to not angle the mouthpiece up or down, aiming straight out.

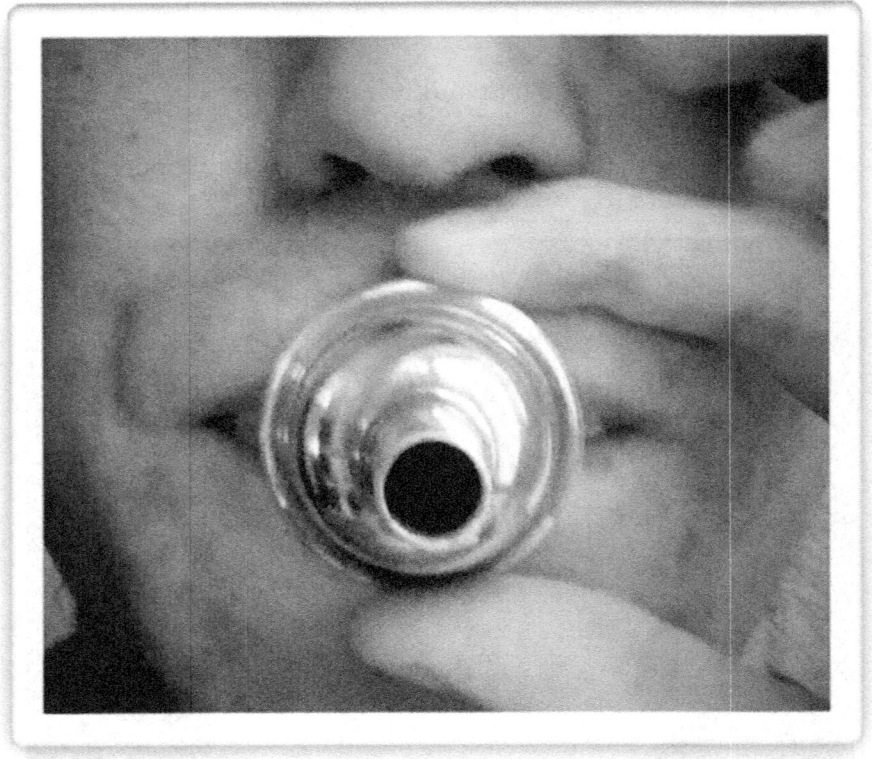

Staying relaxed and letting go of tension is essential. That all said, it's counteractive to overthink your embouchure—once you set yourself and start playing, blow freely and let your air (and ear!) dictate the embouchure.

The slide positions

There are 7 "positions" roughly equidistant along the slide, allowing us to select which note to play.

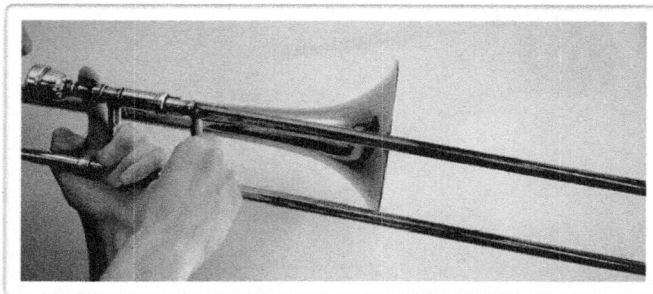

1st
(Slide fully in)

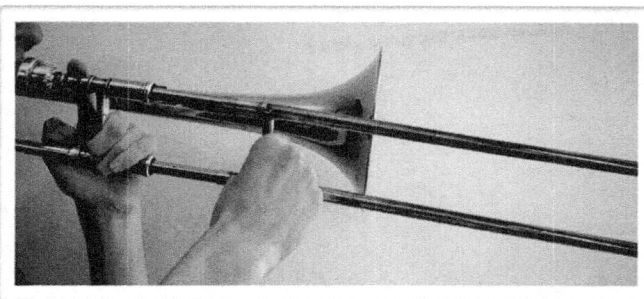

2nd

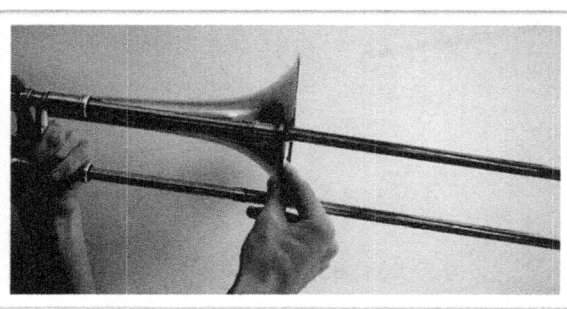

3rd
(Just before the edge of the bell)

How to Play the Trombone

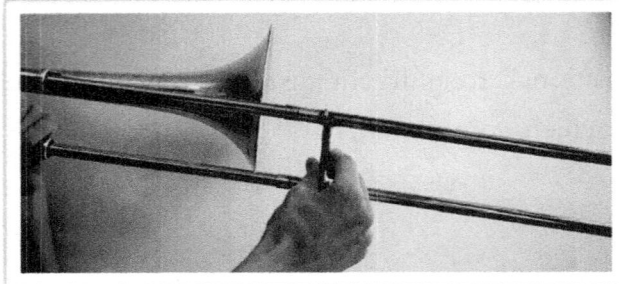

4th
(Just *beyond* the edge of the bell)

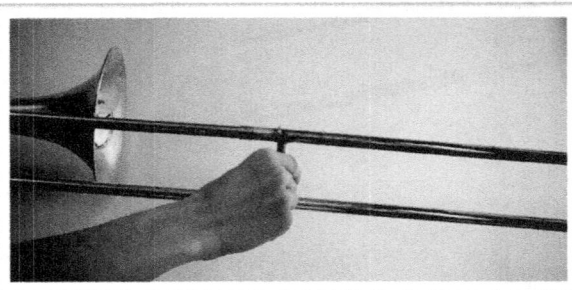

5th

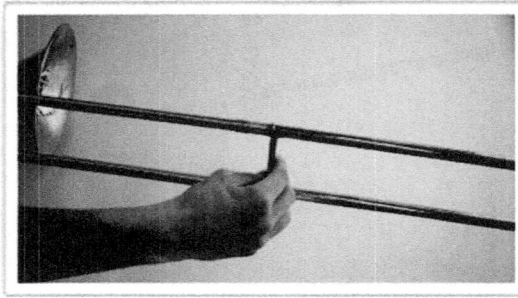

6th

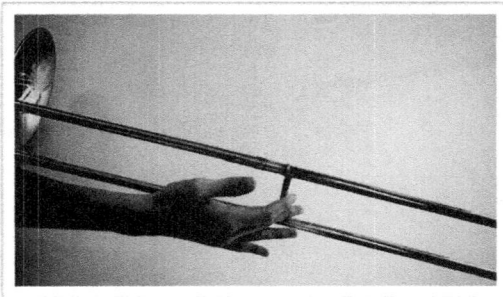

7th
(Right at the end of the slide. Careful not to drop the slide!)

Preparing to Play

The precise location for each position differs slightly across different trombones. Finding the exact position can be tricky, and a little bit of guesswork is involved at the beginning. The authentic way to learn the positions is not with your eyes but *with your ears*. As you work through this book, listen carefully to the audio tracks provided—if you strive to imitate the sound you hear, your ears will lead your hand to the correct position. Trust your ears and you will arrive at each position confidently and crisply!

⭐ Letting your *ears guide you* is a key element of good musicianship ⭐

Understanding the Staff

To read music, you'll first need to know a few basic things about where musical notes are placed. All music is read on what is called a staff. The staff is divided into slices called bars (a.k.a. measures), and consists of five lines and four spaces. Music notes fall somewhere either within these lines and spaces, or even above and below.

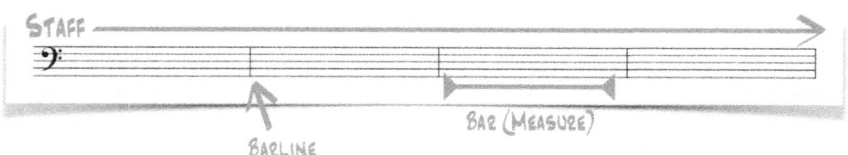

How to Play the Trombone

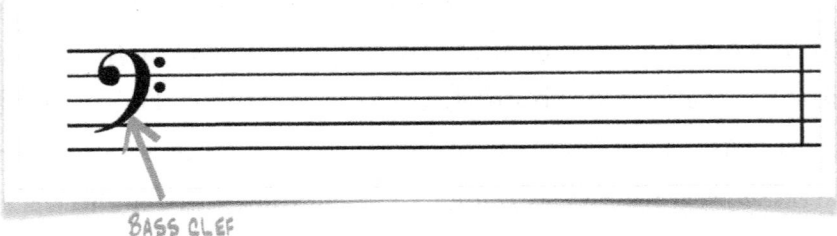

BASS CLEF

Now you're ready to play!

Part Two

Chapter 4

First notes

The note F

Our first goal is to create a nice, steady pitch. We will begin with the note "F". This is what it looks like on a page of music:

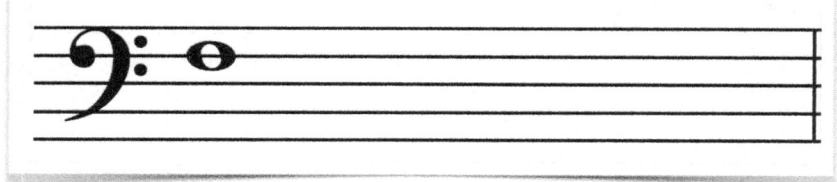

Listening Example #1: Note F

- Listen to the audio first. Then ready your trombone, hold your slide in 1st position (all the way in), and release a big breath of air into the instrument

- Imagine mouthing the word "Tah" as you blow in to help you expel the air cleanly

- Don't worry if no sound comes out initially. It's trickier than you'd expect!

- It helps to imagine that you're blowing *warm air* into the instrument as you mouth "Tah". Remember to maintain the shape of your embouchure!

How to Play the Trombone

Once you get a hang of playing the note, move on to the next.

The note E♭ (pronounced "E flat")

The vertical position of the note (up & down) indicates how high or low a note is. This note, E♭, is a little lower than F.

- Try play it. E♭ is played in 3rd position, the slide placed just before the end of the bell

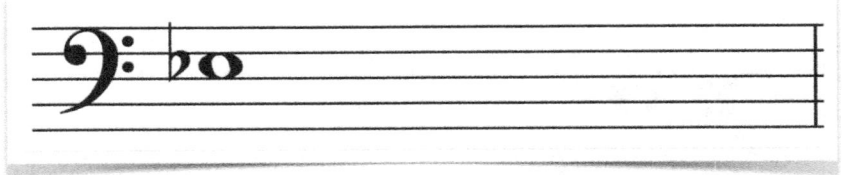

Listening Example #2: Note E♭

The horizontal position (left & right) of a note indicates *when* that note is played. Just like reading English, music notation reads from left to right. So, this example below plays like this: First the note F, then the note E♭.

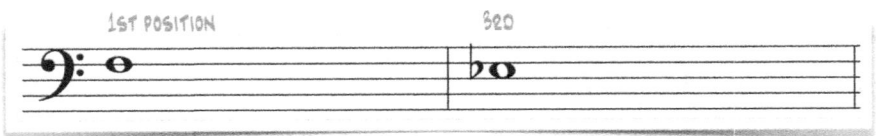

Listening Example #3: F & E♭

- Remember to take a big relaxed breath before each note!

First notes

The note D

Our next note is the note "D". It looks like this, and is played in 4th position.

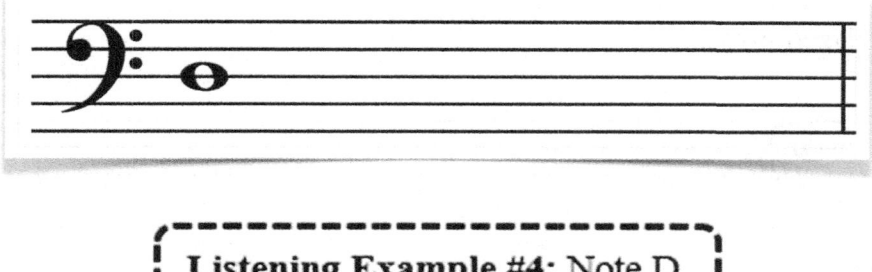

Listening Example #4: Note D

Just like how we use full-stops and commas in English, we use "Rests" in music to punctuate musical sentences. Rests show when there is an *absence of sound,* telling us when not to play.

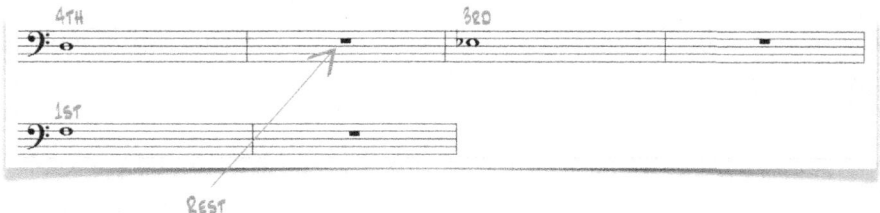

Listening Example #5: D, Eb, & F

- Make sure you become fairly familiar and comfortable with each note and exercise before you move on

The note C

Our next note is the note "C". It looks like this, and is played in 6th position. Make sure to reach the slide out far! Check the note with the audio clip and remember to play the note with the same relaxed breath.

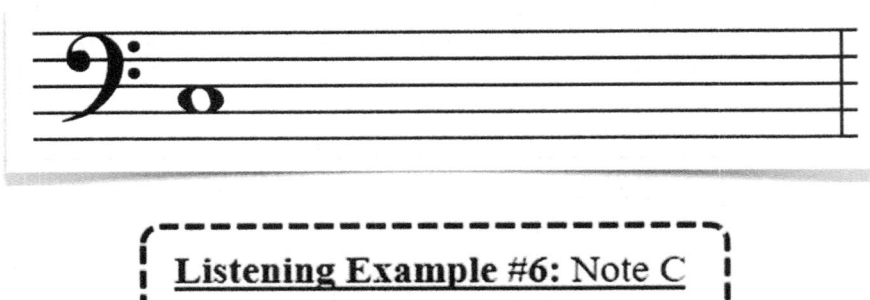

Listening Example #6: Note C

Notes can be played long and slow, and they can be played short and fast—we call these variations "Note lengths". The black notes below are called "Quarter notes" and are played quickly, one note after another.

- Play them with the same big breath, and think "Tah, tah, tah, tah". It may help to first sing out *tah, tah, tah*... away from the trombone.

Listening Example #7: Quarter Notes 1

First notes

- You can take a breath whenever you need air, as long as you are intentional and mindful about your breath when you do

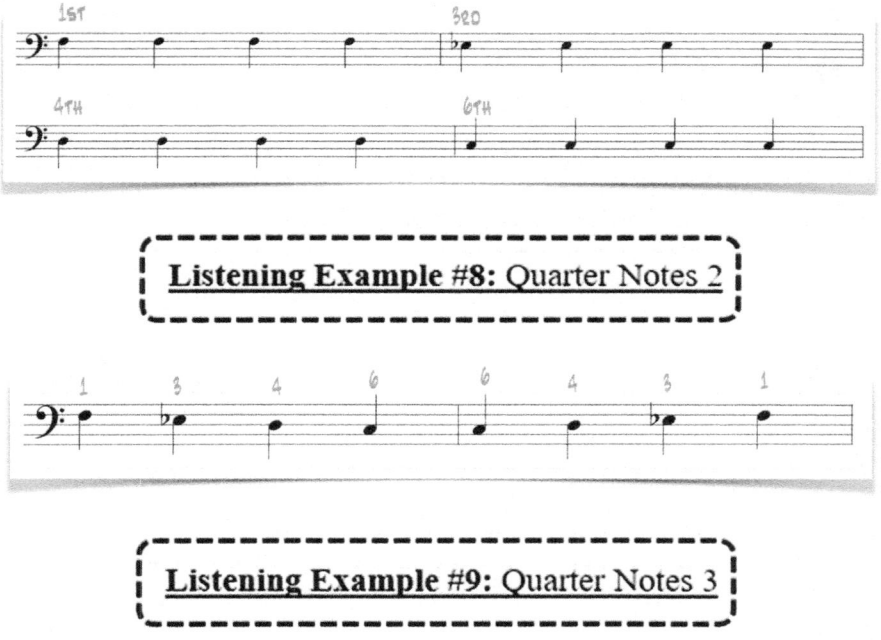

The note B♭

This next note is the note B♭ ("B flat"). It looks like this, and is played in 1st position. You might have just noticed that F and B♭ are both played in 1st position. Let your ear guide your mouth (embouchure!) and breath. It helps to think *slower and warmer air* to sound this low B♭ note.

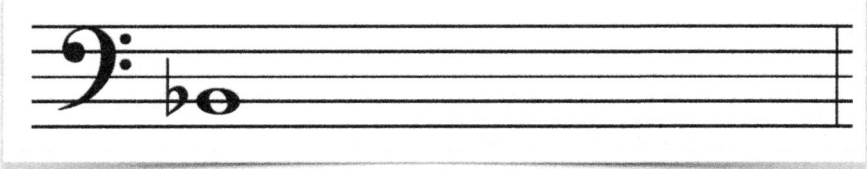

How to Play the Trombone

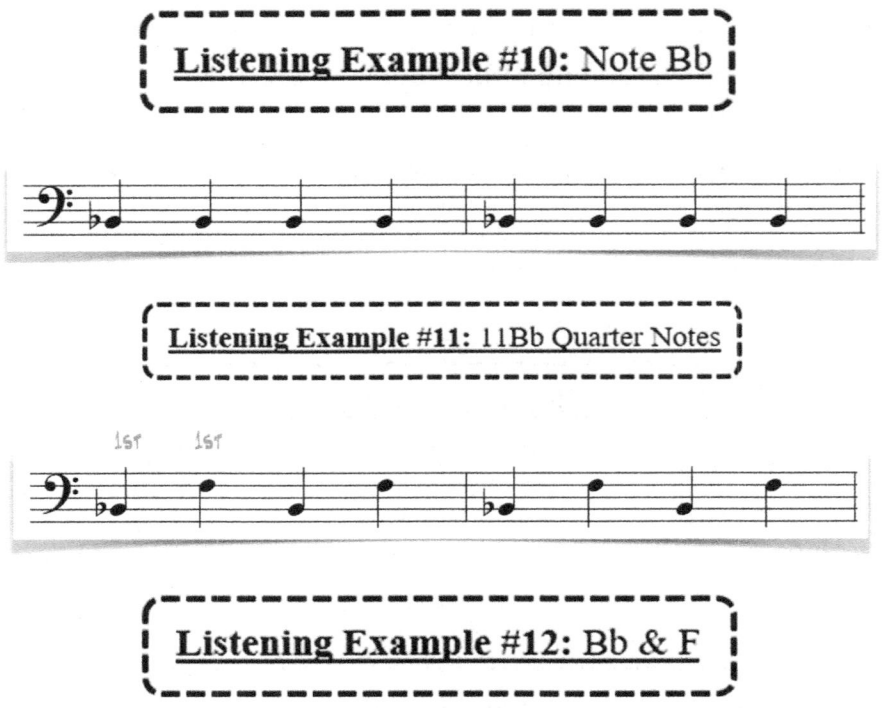

There are quarter notes, and there are also *quarter note rests*. These rests span the same length of time that quarter notes do. Check with the audio recording to hear and feel these rhythms.

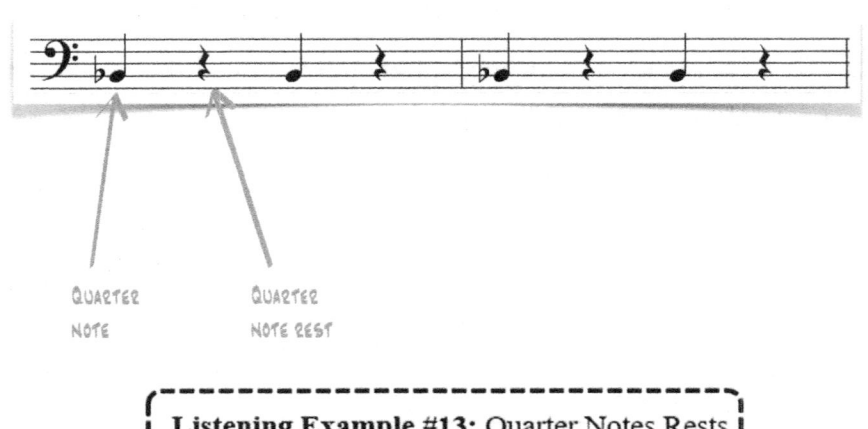

First notes

First Song

You're ready to play your first song! You may recognize this melody. Remember your big relaxed breath.

Listening Example #14: First Song

- Feel free to play along with the recordings, or play by yourself

Keep returning to earlier exercises to strengthen the notes we've learned so far. We'll push on with some higher notes—they take a little bit of getting used to, so don't be discouraged if they don't speak right away.

The note G

This is the note G. It's a little higher than F, the first note we learned. G is played in 4th position.

- Use a strong and fast airflow to support higher notes

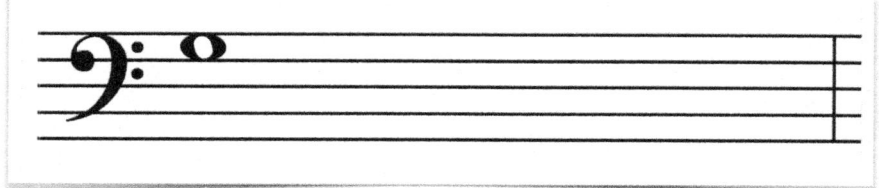

How to Play the Trombone

Listening Example #15: Note G

- Half notes are another type of note-length. They are not quite as rapid as quarter notes.

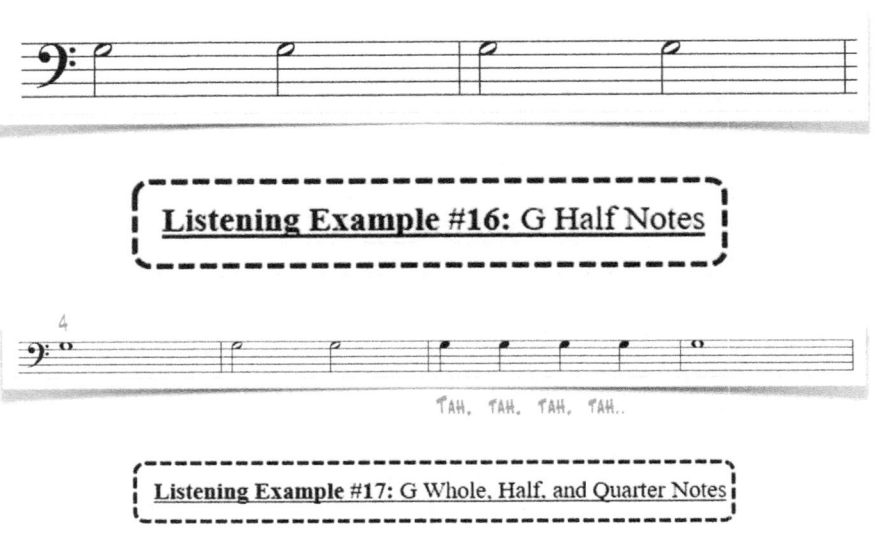

Listening Example #16: G Half Notes

Listening Example #17: G Whole, Half, and Quarter Notes

Twinkle Twinkle Little Star

First notes

- This "time signature" simply reminds us that each bar (measure) contains 4 quarter notes

> **Listening Example #18:** Twinkle Twinkle Little Star

The note A

One step higher we have the note A, played in 2nd position.

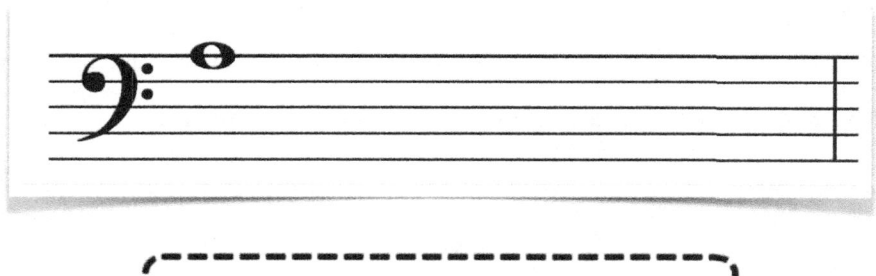

> **Listening Example #19:** Note A

- These are half note *rests*, the gap in sound taking up the same length of time that half *notes* do.

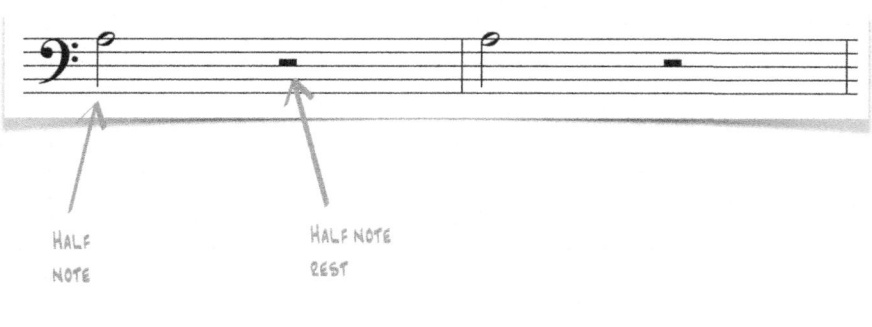

> **Listening Example #20:** A Half Notes Rests

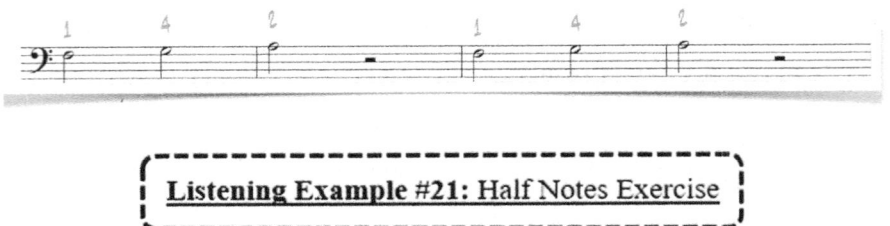

> **Listening Example #21: Half Notes Exercise**

The note B♭ (B flat)

We arrive at B♭. Keep in mind that this is a different note from the low B♭ we learned earlier. It's played in 1st position just like the low B♭, sounds the same, but *feels* higher and brighter.

- Support this note with a big breath and fast air, making sure to remain relaxed and controlled

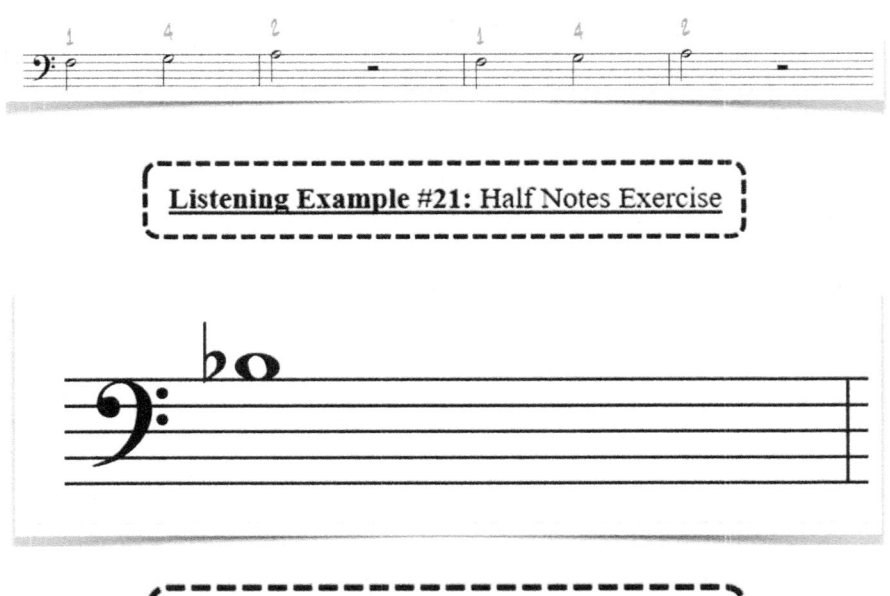

> **Listening Example #21: Half Notes Exercise**

> **Listening Example #22: Note B♭**

First notes

Listening Example #23: Note Bb Exercise 1

Listening Example #24: Note Bb Exercise 2

Listening Example #25: Note Bb Exercise 3

Another Piece

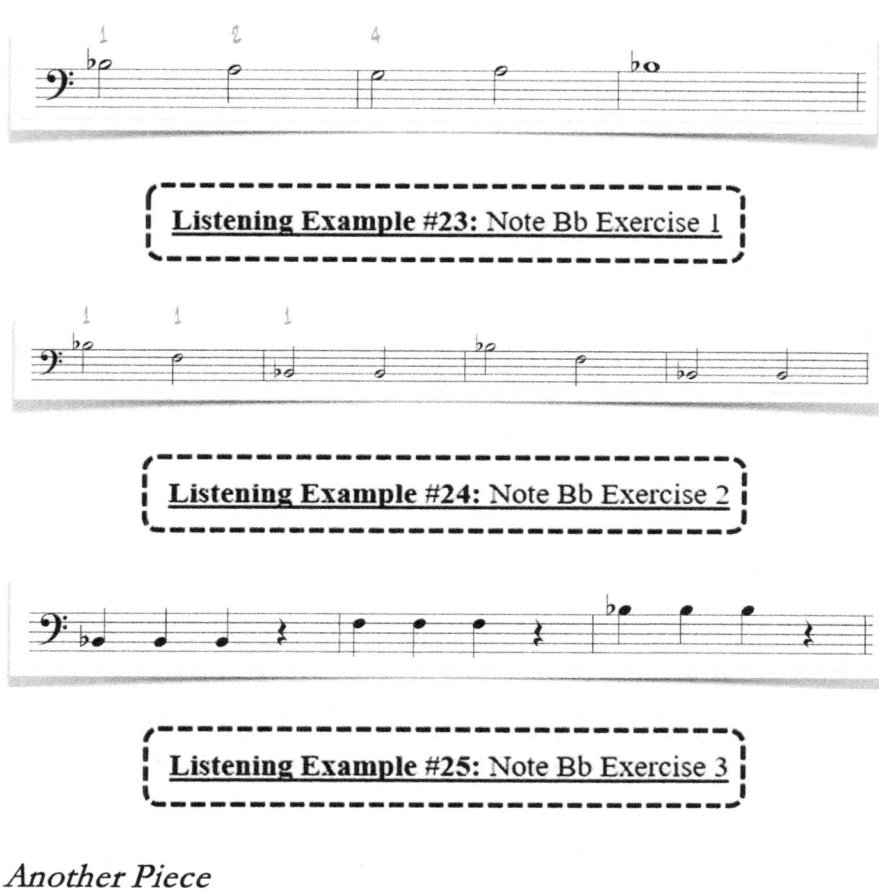

Listening Example #26: Another Piece

B♭ scale

All of the notes we've learned so far combine to form the B♭ scale. A "Scale" is a set sequence of notes. Play this example, the B♭ scale, as smoothly and cleanly as you can. The aim is to *clone* each note so that all notes have the same quality of sound.

- Learn this scale up and down, inside and out, even memorized so you know it like the back of your hand. Absorb the sound of the entire line of notes as a whole

Listening Example #27: B♭ Scale

Chapter 5

Next Steps and Beyond

Low A

Our next note to learn is low A, found on the bottom of the staff. We play this note in the same as the higher A, 2nd position. Think *slow air,* and avoid relaxing so much to the point where it feels flabby.

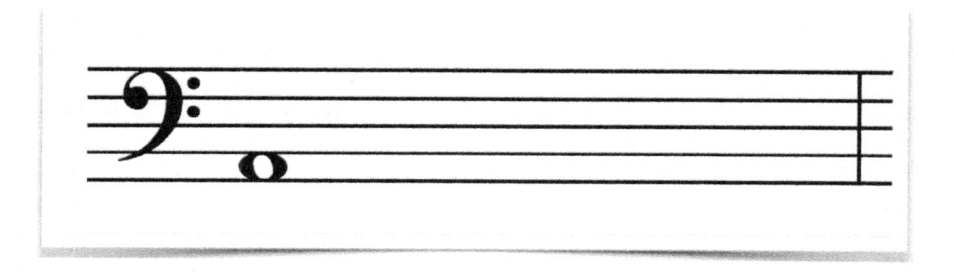

Listening Example #28: Low A

Music can be loud and big, or quiet and soft. We use markings to instruct these volume changes in music: "*p*" for *piano* means softly, "*f*" for *forte* means loud. We call these levels of loudnesses the *dynamics*.

- Play the next example keeping close attention to the changes in dynamics for loud and soft. Support the *forte* sections with plenty of air, and blow a contained and controlled airflow for the *piano* sections.

How to Play the Trombone

(musical notation with f marked "LOUD" and p marked "QUIET")

Listening Example #29: Forte & Piano

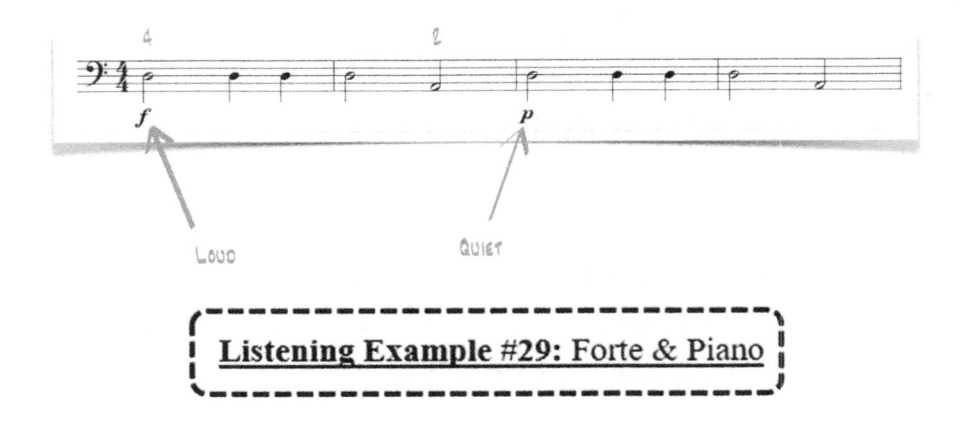

Middle C

This note is C, played in third position. Support this high note with a strong, confident airflow. It may take quite a few tries as it requires more control of the air than the lower notes. It's okay if you don't quite get the note initially—what's most important is to remain relaxed when playing

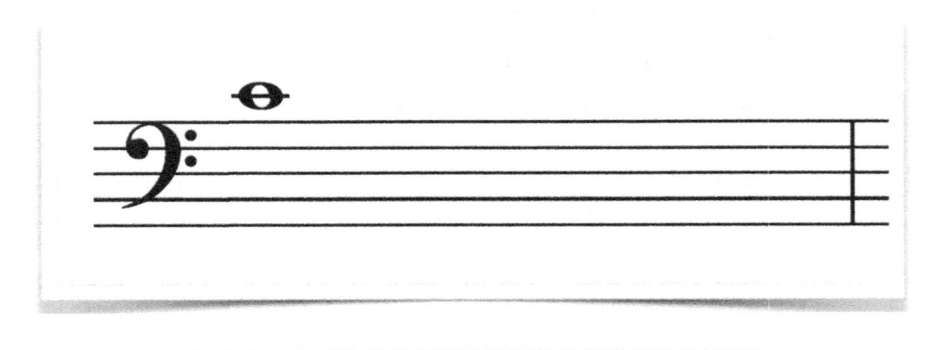

Listening Example #30: Middle C

Next Steps and Beyond

Often we like to change between dynamics (volume levels) gradually rather than suddenly. To do this we use what we call "Hairpins". The shape (< or >) guides the performer through the dynamic change. The wider the hairpin, the louder you play. The narrower, the quieter.

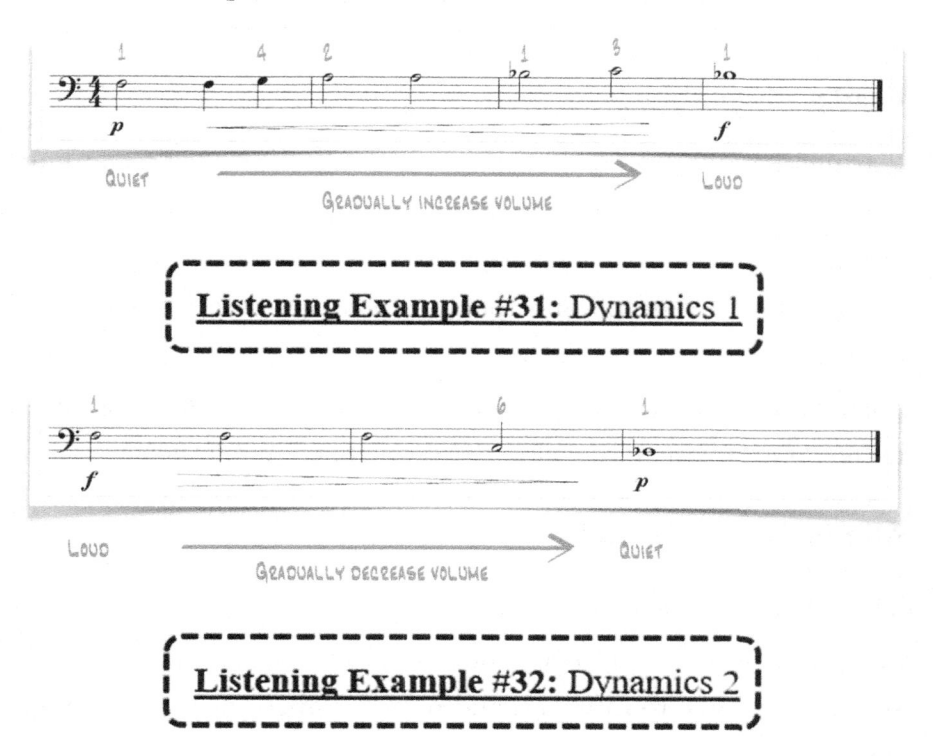

*[Musical notation: bass clef, 4/4, showing notes with *p* marking, crescendo hairpin to *f*, labeled "QUIET — GRADUALLY INCREASE VOLUME → LOUD"]*

Listening Example #31: Dynamics 1

*[Musical notation: bass clef, showing notes with *f* marking, decrescendo hairpin to *p*, labeled "LOUD — GRADUALLY DECREASE VOLUME → QUIET"]*

Listening Example #32: Dynamics 2

We can use hairpins over single long notes, too.

- Explore the strength of your air, the tightness of your embouchure to achieve a smooth rising and falling of dynamic, maintaining the same quality of sound no matter how loud or quiet

> **Listening Example #33: Dynamics 3**

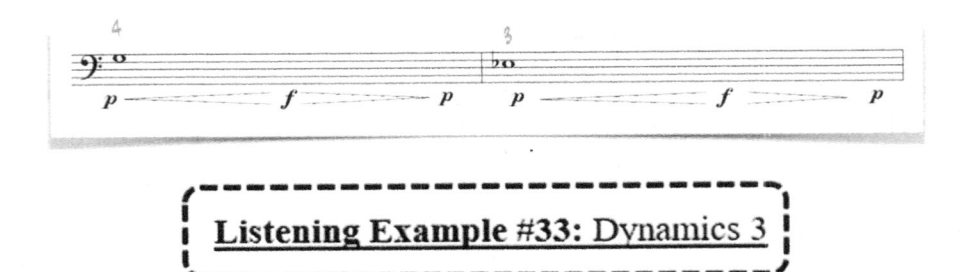

Fearless High Notes

Playing high notes on the trombone is a challenging but rewarding pursuit. Use plenty of fast moving air, supporting the note all the way through. The trick to getting good at playing high notes is to spend a lot of time playing them, as well as going beyond your comfort zones and boundaries. Take care not to force it, avoid pushing the instrument into your face or use too much tension—it takes a long time to develop nice controlled high notes!

Middle D and Beyond

This D, sitting above the staff, is played in 1st position. E♭ is in 3rd position, F in 1st. These notes will take some experience to sound—feel free to move on and return to these notes at another time.

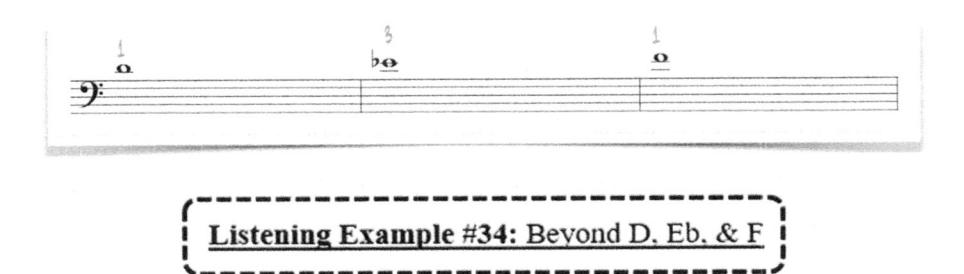

> **Listening Example #34: Beyond D, E♭, & F**

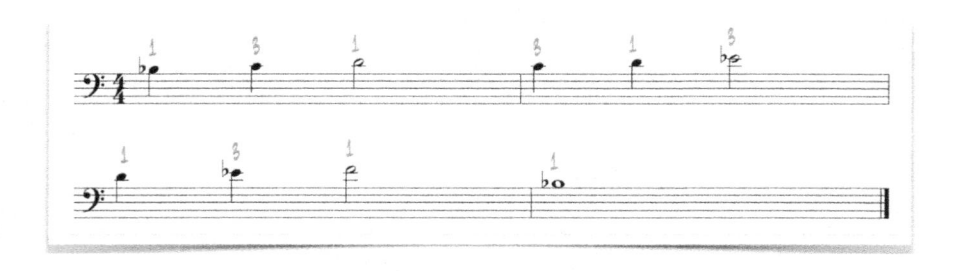

Listening Example #35: D, Eb, & F

Low G and F

Low notes have a different character of sound, but the same concepts we use for high notes still apply. A steady airflow and control of the embouchure is required as to avoid a "flabby" note. Low G is played in 4th, while low F is played in 6th position. Again, these notes require some experience before they start to sound and feel good.

Listening Example #36: Low G & F

- Play the next example carefully, prioritizing control over speed

Listening Example #37: Low Little Lamb

Eighth note rhythms are played twice as quickly as quarter notes.

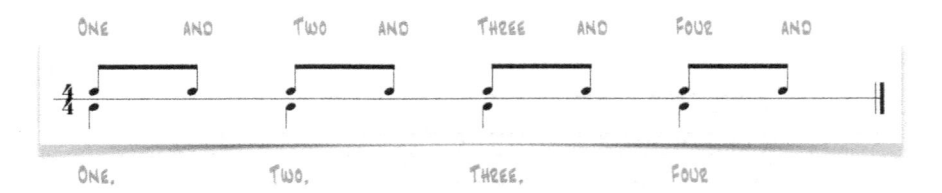

- Make sure to move your slide quickly and smoothly and arrive at each position, without ambiguity.

Listening Example #38: 8th Note Tune

⭐ The way to practice fast and complex music is to practice it slowly first ⭐

Listening Example #39: 8th Note Tune 2

Tempo

Music of many forms have a pulse. Just like a heartbeat, this consistent pulse carries music across time whether it be fast or slow. We call this pulse the music's *tempo*.

- Play the above example again, with the new audio. You'll hear a tool called a metronome "Clicking" along to the music relentlessly. This clicking is the literal representation the tempo that we feel internally to carry us through the music.

Listening Example #40: 8th Note Tune 2 with Metronome

The notes and musical building blocks learned so far will give you plenty of milage for the music you will encounter as a trombonist. Make sure to keep returning to practice all of the exercises, strengthening each note and song until they become comfortable and effortless to play.

Chapter 6

More to play

Glissing

Blowing whist moving the slide is called a gliss. It sounds fun and can be a great exercise for your slide arm as well as your breath.

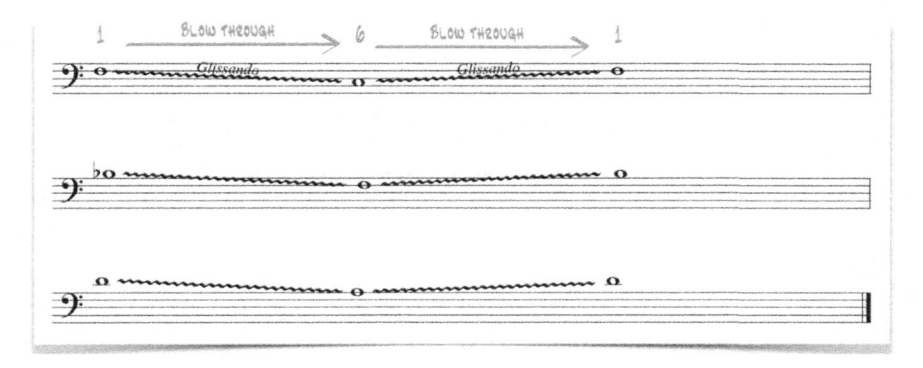

Listening Example #41: Glissing

Slurs

Changing note without re-articulating the note is called a lip slur. Try these exercises that challenge your *flexibility*, which is your ability to smoothly move from note to note in the same position all within the same breath.

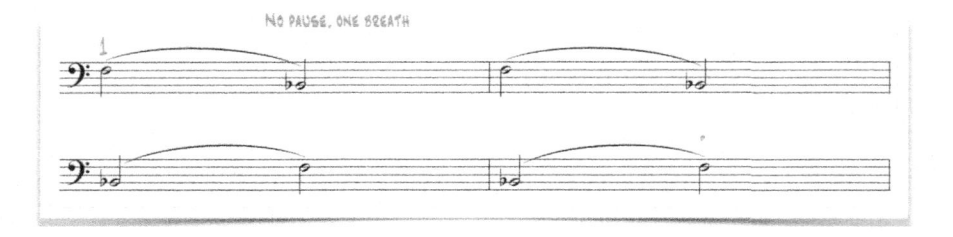

How to Play the Trombone

Listening Example #42: Slurs 1

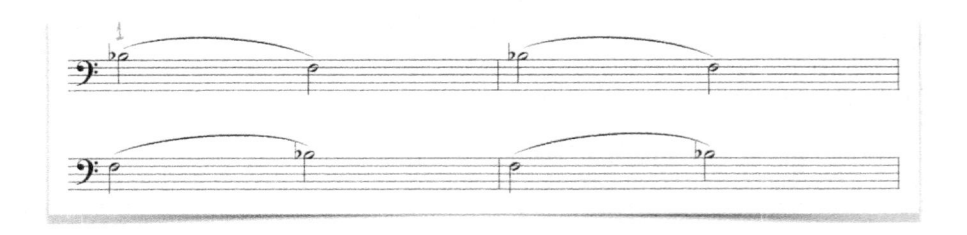

Listening Example #43: Slurs 2

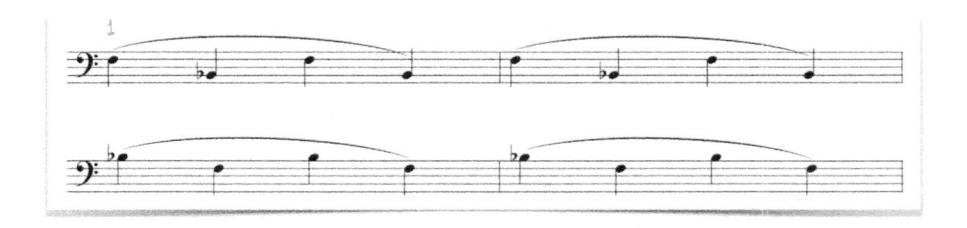

Listening Example #44: Slurs 3

- Try these exercises in every slide position!

More to play

Saints

(Key Signature)

Listening Example #45: Saints

- In the above piece, you'll notice a flat sign (♭) placed at the beginning of each staff, placed specifically on the B line in this example. This tells us that every B note in the piece is flattened to the B *flat* note. This is called the *key signature* and it saves needing to place a flat sign (♭) in front of every single note. More on reading music next.

Chapter 7

More Theory and the Musical Alphabet

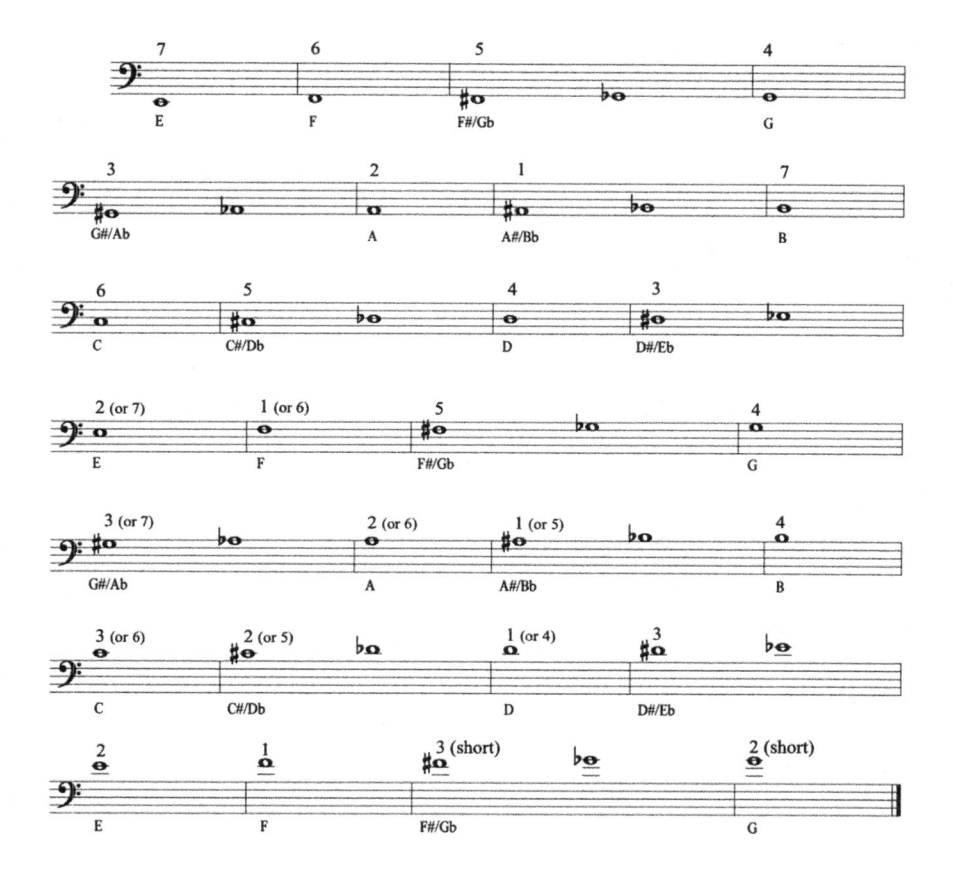

Slide Position Chart

Some notes have the option to be played in more than one position. These alternate positions can be handy to know, but focus on learning one position per note at first.

Sharps and Flats (a.k.a. "Accidentals")

- The musical alphabet reads from A to G, then starting again at A and continuing (ABCDEFGABCDE...)

- There are some extra notes between each letter, however: For example, the note *in-between* G and A is called G♯, equally read as A♭

- ♯ = Sharp. <u>Raises</u> the note. G♯ is a note a step *up* from G

- ♭ = Flat. <u>Lowers</u> the note. G♭ is a note a step *down* from G

- When a particular note needs to be specified that it's *neither* a ♯ or ♭, we call it a *natural* note, using the symbol ♮

- G♯, G(♮) and G♭ are three different notes

Tips for Reading Notes on the Staff

Learn these mnemonics to help you remember and quickly recognize the note names laid on the staff:

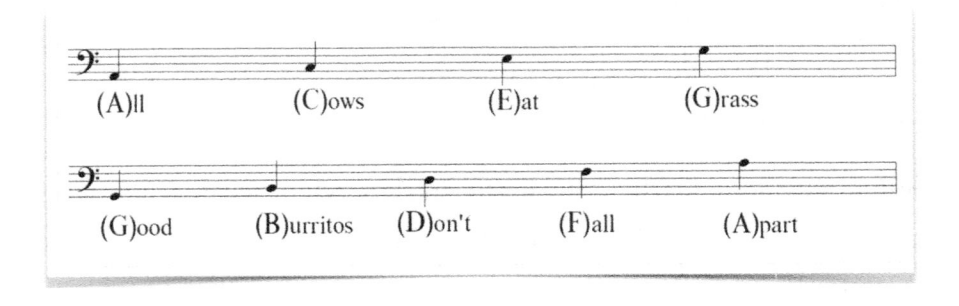

(A)ll　　(C)ows　　(E)at　　(G)rass

(G)ood　(B)urritos　(D)on't　(F)all　(A)part

More Theory and the Musical Alphabet

Notes above the staff:

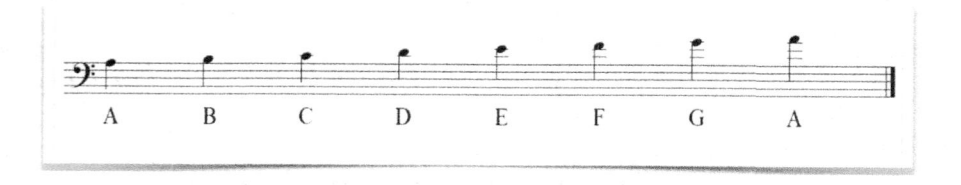

A B C D E F G A

Using the F-trigger

Your trombone might have some extra tubing and a switch attached. This is the "F-trigger", a mechanism that allows you to change notes without moving the slide. This trigger helps with reaching the far positions easily, and it also extends how low your trombone can play.

"T1" means slide position 1 along with the trigger engaged. "Long" means the slide position is actually slightly further away than usual.

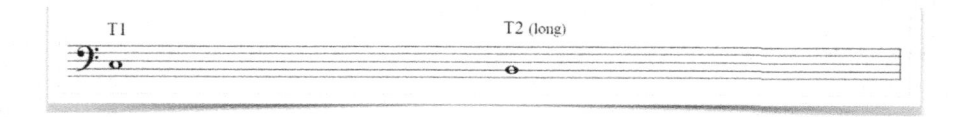

T1   T2 (long)

Extra low notes playable with the F-trigger:

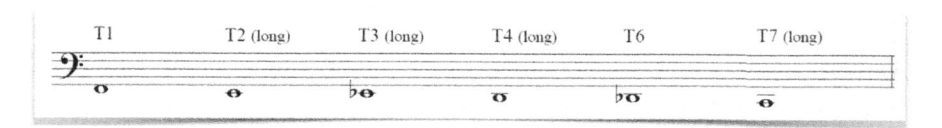

T1   T2 (long)   T3 (long)   T4 (long)   T6   T7 (long)

Visualizing Rhythm

Listen to the audio example to help you hear these rhythms:

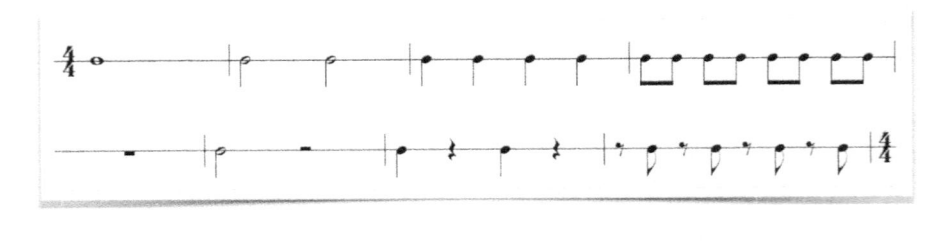

Listening Example #46: Rhythm Example

Ties connect two or more notes (ie. tying them together), elongating the note. Ties can join all kinds notes together, regardless of if they are in same measure or across bar lines.

More Dynamics

"m" stands for "Moderato" in Italian, as in *moderately quiet—mp* or *moderately loud—mf*

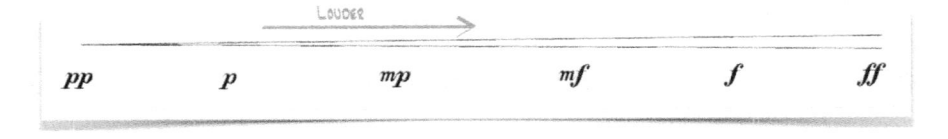

Articulations

To "articulate" is to express an idea fluently. In music, we can express the same phrase in different ways. To do this on the trombone, we use our tongue to shape each note uniquely. Listen to and play these examples, noticing how the character of the exact

More Theory and the Musical Alphabet

same melody can completely change just by applying different *articulations* to them.

- *Staccato*, signified by a small dot above the note, means play the note short. Mouth the word "tu" as you blow staccato notes

Listening Example #47: Staccato

- *Tenuto*, signified by a horizontal line, means play the note long. Articulate these notes with the word "dah"

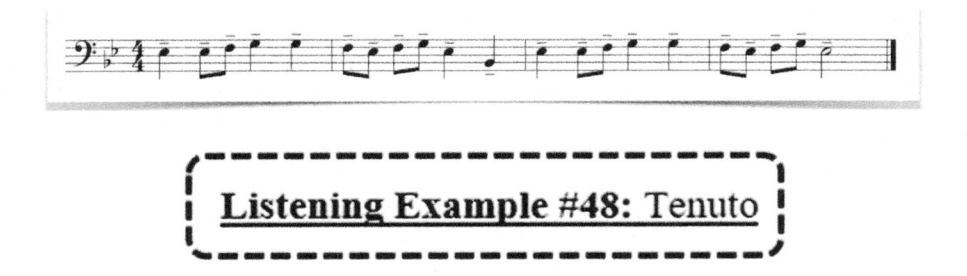

Listening Example #48: Tenuto

- *Accent*, signified by a sideways "v", means put extra force into the attack of the note

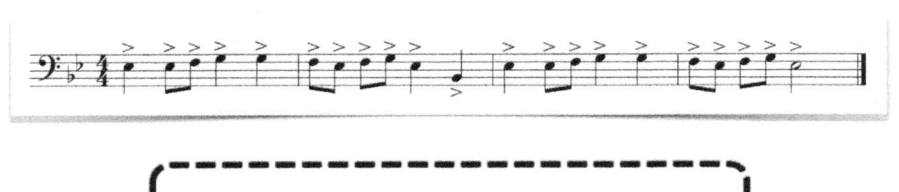

Listening Example #49: Accent

How to Play the Trombone

- Phrase marks show where each musical "sentence" begins and ends. Play smoothly through each phrase, not taking a breath until the end of each phrase.

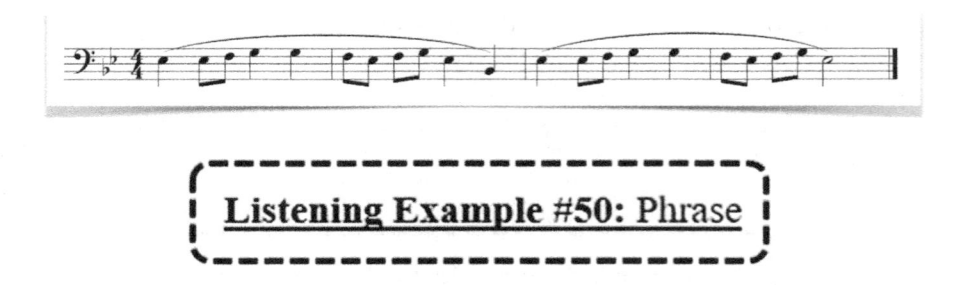

Listening Example #50: Phrase

- Articulations often combine, shaping the melody

- Repeat signs are used when a musical passage is desired to be played again the exact same way, just like a loop

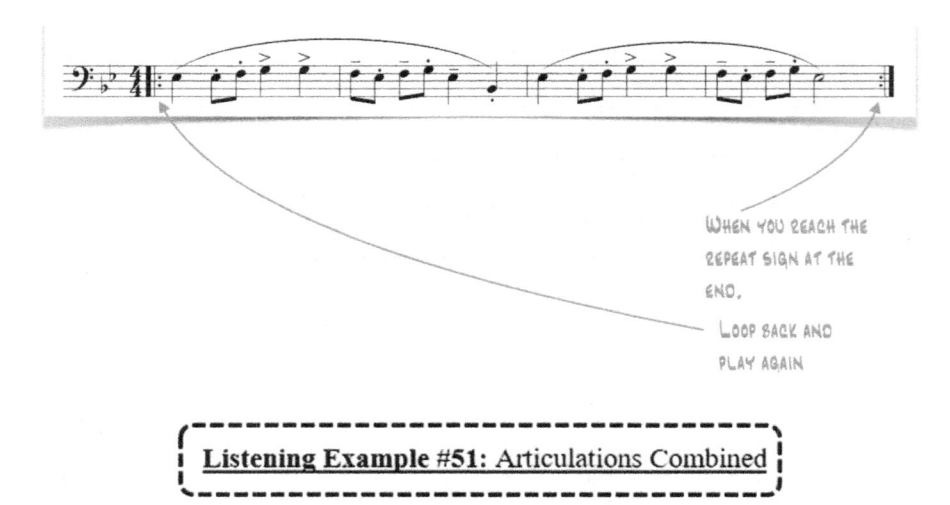

WHEN YOU REACH THE REPEAT SIGN AT THE END, LOOP BACK AND PLAY AGAIN

Listening Example #51: Articulations Combined

Part Three

Chapter 8

General Info

Troubleshooting

- Mouthpieces can sometimes get stuck in the receiver of the trombone, making it frustratingly difficult to free. It's important to refrain from forcing, levering or twisting anything to try pull it out. If it remains stuck despite some gentle convincing, a music store assistant will be more than happy to release your mouthpiece with a special tool

- Though it is ideal to keep the instrument from bumping into objects and furniture, it is probable that you will hit and dent your instrument every now and then. The most important component to protect is the slide. Slides can dent easily, which can then make playing the trombone uncomfortable or even impossible. Your local music store should be equipped to deal with smoothening out these dents. While they're at it, they may also offer to smooth out any dents found elsewhere on the trombone, such as the bell or the tuning slide. Dents in those areas can be unsightly, but are relatively harmless to the playing and sound of the instrument

- Water key springs can snap, just from regular use over time. Replacement springs are readily available, which you can install yourself if so inclined. While waiting on the new spring, you can use a rubber band to maintain the air seal of the water key

Purchasing a Trombone

Deciding which instrument to purchase can be a daunting experience with all the brands, models, prices and conditions available to you. A good rule is to stay within the well known brands. Going to a store in person and handling the instruments yourself is a worthwhile experience as well.

Yamaha, Bach, Conn, King, Getzen, Kanstul are brands that offer reliable instruments. More premium companies such as Rath, Edwards, Shires, Eastman and BAC often offer beginner and intermediate grade models within their product lines that can also be recommended.

Buying used or renting an instrument is a competitive option. Used trombones are a great option because they offer virtually the same quality of instrument as if you buy new. Again, it's worth playing an instrument made by a trusted brand, rather than buying new from a cheap and nameless brand. To buy used, it's recommended to purchase in person to see the instrument and inspect its physical condition. Making sure the instrument has a smooth slide and has no leaks are the things to check for. They may have some cosmetic wear, such as the shiny lacquer having rubbed off, but that won't affect how it plays—it just shows that the instrument has been loved!

Plastic trombones are the lightweight and colorfully built alternatives to their metallic cousins. Whilst they aren't built quite to the same quality or sound, they still play well and offer an affordable and less fragile beginner-targeted alternative to instruments made of brass. pBone and Tromba are the established

General Info

brands. One tip with playing plastic trombones is to upgrade from their plastic mouthpieces and use a standard brass mouthpiece.

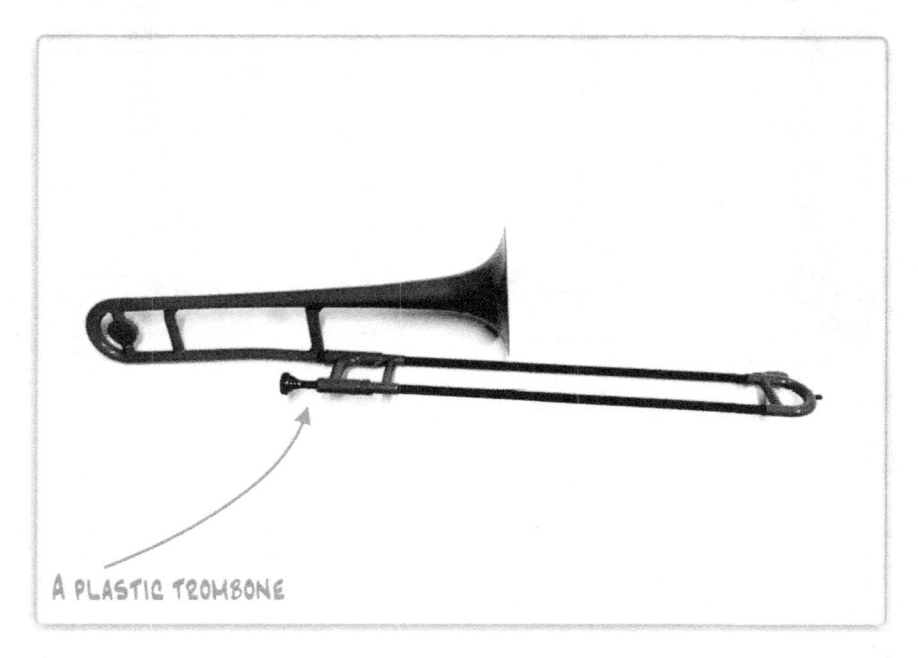

A PLASTIC TROMBONE

Mouthpieces come in all shapes and sizes, but don't worry, they'll all work and many trombones come included with one. They are divided into two "shank" size categories, one designed for smaller trombones and another for larger trombones. Your mouthpiece is compatible with any trombone, as long as the shank sizes match!

There is a whole world of mouthpiece styles and dimensions. A good starting point would be to begin by playing a smaller mouthpiece, as in a mouthpiece with small cup (depth) and rim (width) dimensions. Different brands use different naming conventions but a ubiquitous small shank mouthpiece is the Bach 12C, whilst the Bach 6½ is often used with large shank trombones. There's no need to get too caught in the numbers however, anything included with your trombone will play well!

General Care

- Keep the slide slick and smooth, applying oil and spraying water as needed.

- Whilst not essential, using a slide rod is a great way to keep your slide in top condition. Essentially a thin stick attached to cloth, cleaning the inside of the outer slide can dramatically improve the slickness of the slide.

- Make sure to rinse your mouthpiece every few days

- Every few months, reapply some grease on the tuning slide to prevent it from becoming stuck

Deep Cleaning

The most recommended way to deep clean your trombone is by giving it a bath! Fill your bath with lukewarm water (some say to add a little bit of dishwashing liquid). Pull your trombone apart into all it's pieces and soak, lining the floor of the bathtub with a towel to protect the tub and your trombone. Gently scrubbing the nooks and crannies with a rag or toothbrush can clear away the grime that builds up over time. It's recommended to give your trombone a deep clean once per year or so.

Mutes

Mutes are musical accessories that insert right in to the end of the bell of the trombone, changing the timbre (sound) of the trombone as well as dampening the overall volume of the instrument. Some music may ask specifically for these mutes, but they are not necessary for a beginning player. They are fairly inexpensive however, so you're welcome to explore these fun sounds as you develop as a trombonist.

- Cup

Commonly used across many genres, cup mutes soften the blasty sound of the trombone and projects a rounder sound.

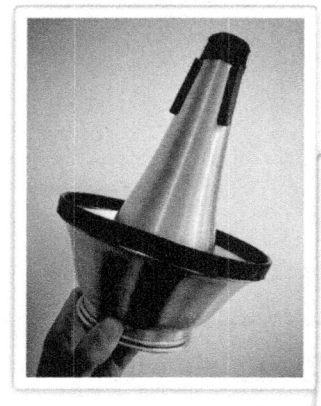

> **Listening Example #52: Cup Mute**

- Straight

The most simplistic of all the mutes, straight mutes project well, often giving the trombone sound a dry or metallic quality.

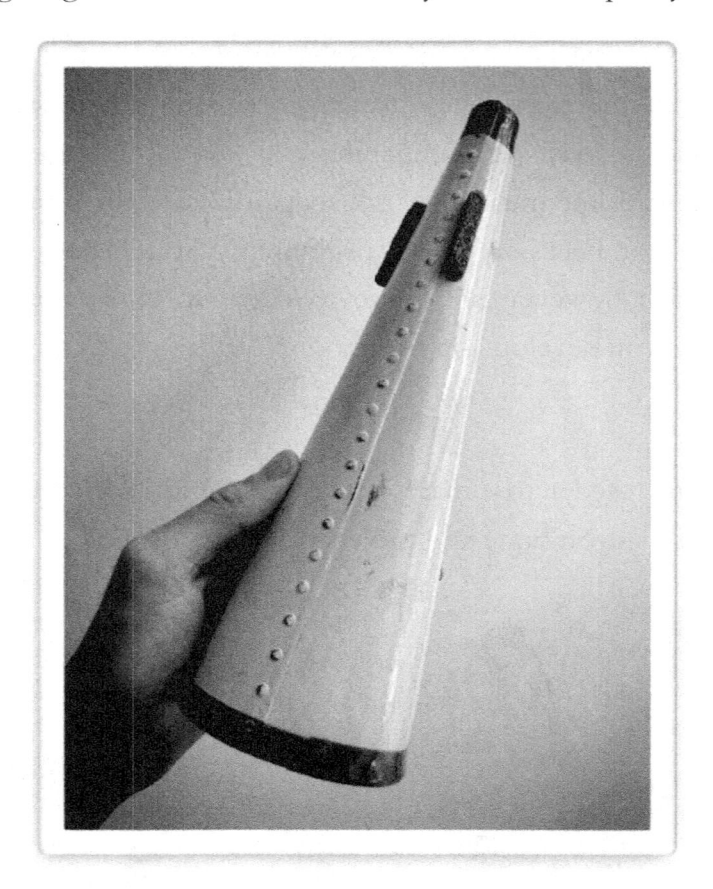

> **Listening Example #53: Straight Mute**

General Info

- Bucket

These mutes cover a large portion of the bell opening and are often lined with fabric-like material, creating a warm, fuzzy and subdued tone.

Listening Example #54: Bucket Mute

- Harmon

Perhaps one of the least used mutes, harmon mutes feature a stem that is inserted inside the mute which gives out a colorful tone.

- Plunger

Most often used in jazz music and also made famous for it's role in the sad trombone sound effect ("Wah-wah…"). Musicians often use a regular toilet plunger from the hardware store! Commonly used in tandem with a pixie mute, a thin style straight mute that goes deep into the bell.

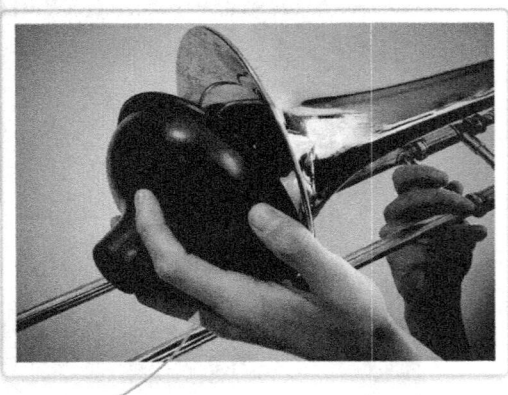

Plunger mutes are unique because they are held in the hand while playing. The ability to open and close the mute gives great variety and personality to the sound

Listening Example #55: Plunger Mute

General Info

- Practise

Unlike the other mutes above, these mutes are not intended for performance but are designed solely to minimize the volume of sound as much as possible, so you can still practice when and where you need to be quiet. Some even feature microphones inside, letting you plug your headphones in so that only you can hear your trombone at full volume. These are not a complete replacement for practicing mute-free, but can be useful in a pinch.

Breathing Exercises

Sometimes it can be useful to try some exercises to reacquaint and refocus with your breath.

Lots of fun paraphernalia are available to help visualize and train your lungs, though they are not required.
Breathing bags (essentially a durable rubber sack) are the most commonly used. They help prevent hyperventilation so one can practice breathing without getting dizzy.

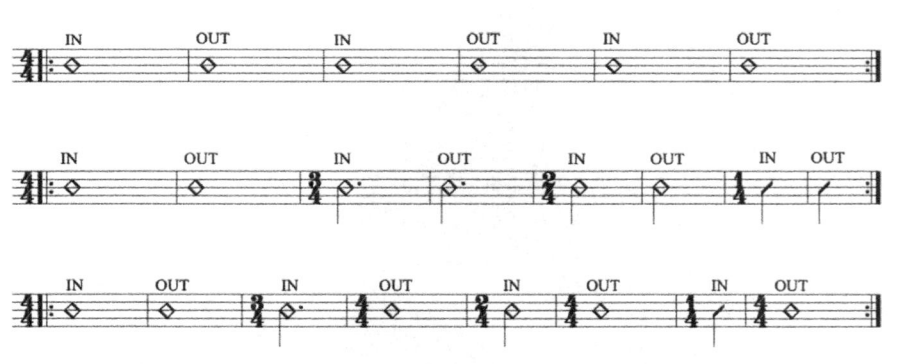

- Sit tall and fill your lungs to maximum

- Breathe without stress nor friction, striving for a dark and quiet sound as the air rushes past your lips

Chapter 9

Send Off

Artists to Discover

The world of the trombone is a vast and wide ranging collection of players old and new, full of innovators as well as supporting artists. Below is just a small list of trombone players famous across multiple genres of music.

- **Joe Alessi** and **Christian Lindberg** are virtuoso classical musicians, famous for their solos and concerto performances

- **JJ Johnson** and **Melba Liston** and are a couple of the great jazz players that brought the instrument to fame

- From Brazil, **Raul de Souza** brought his valve trombone sound to the funk and dance genre

- **Trombone Shorty** is a modern trombonist (and trumpeter + vocalist!) infusing his home town New Orleans sound with funk and pop influences

The trombone can also be often heard in backing band roles supporting featured artists.

- The music of **Michael Jackson, Stevie Wonder, Beyoncé, Bruno Mars** and **Bad Bunny** to name a few use "Horn sections" that include trombones

- You'll be sure to see some trombones at your nearest symphony orchestra and jazz big band shows. The trombone is also often heard playing in reggae bands, trombone choirs, ska bands, salsa bands and more!

Learning Music by Ear

A unique approach to learning a piece of music is imitating what you hear, figuring out the notes with nothing but your ears. This is a fun and effective way of developing your musicianship, strengthening your understanding of music and developing a keen intuition for impromptu music making (Improvising).

A great starting point would be to find music you like, feel excited by and familiar with. It may be a pop song or even a commercial jingle, played by any instrument or voice. Playing the song back on the trombone is the challenge. It may take a little getting used to at first, but if you take it slowly, note by note, you'll start to hear the phrases and notes quite clearly and be able to perform it naturally!

☆ As you get better and better at playing the trombone, it's helpful to imagine that the trombone is not the instrument anymore—the instrument is you! The trombone merely becomes an extension, a loudspeaker amplifying your musical intuition. Gaining more technique on the instrument is important as it allows us to speak our ideas more clearly ☆

Conclusion

We hope you got a taste of the trombone and the practicing process. The information found in this book is just the tip of the iceberg, a small sample of the extensive world of music and techniques possible on the trombone.

Perhaps you just needed some basic knowledge, in which case we hope you grasped the foundational concepts covered throughout these pages. Or maybe this is the beginning of a long-lasting musical adventure. If you found the process of this book exciting and you are feeling inspired to learn more, here are some suggestions for your potential next steps:

- Explore the myriad of performance and instructional videos found online. Seeing the trombone being played visually can be an immensely useful tool in learning

- For the extra ambitious book learners, the Arban's Book may be the challenging next step in your practicing journey. The Arban's is a famous encyclopedia of musical exercises written well over a century ago and is still used by professionals today. Full of exercises and songs, it began as a book for cornet/trumpet players which has since been converted for practicing on the trombone. Many other exercise and song books are out there, and the author recommends exploring them too

- Lastly, a great idea is to find a private teacher near you, someone you can meet with on a semi-regular basis. Once you find one that you feel excited to work with, tutors can be a great motivator, helping you to continue your musical journey.

If you've enjoyed reading this book, subscribe* to my mailing list for exclusive content and sneak peeks of my future books.

Visit the link below:

http://eepurl.com/duJ-yf

OR

Use the QR Code:

(*Must be 13 years or older to subscribe)

Made in the USA
Las Vegas, NV
15 November 2023